BLACK GUIDE TO MONEY

101 Secret Ways to Make Money Online

L.L. Maiden

Produced by: Kenneth Chambliss Jr.
Interior design by: Reanna Maiden
Edited by: Regina Maiden

ISBN: 1477473491
ISBN-13: **978-1477473498**

Printed in the United States of America

DEDICATION

This book is dedicated to the youth.
May they go further than we ever could dream.

CONTENTS

ACKNOWLEDGMENTS

Self-sufficiency should start at home. I am eternally grateful to my family for being brave enough to live an unconventional life. To my dad and grandmother, for showing me what entrepreneurship looks like from a young age. My mother, who has never doubted me. To my fiancé, for being open-minded enough to accept the fact that I'm not built for a traditional 9 to 5. Your consistent encouragement fuels me. My younger siblings, I strive to be someone you can look up to. To all the business owners I've met throughout the past years, I thank you for unknowingly inspiring my personal journey. To anyone who has ever had a dream, you can be fearless enough to make it into a reality. This book is a tribute to you.

CHAPTER 1
WHY SHOULD YOU START AN ONLINE BUSINESS ANYWAY?

If you've ever wondered how to start your own website, or how to make money using the internet, look no further! You've just opened your golden ticket to success. In this book you will learn all the secrets to starting your own online business in a simple, yet straight to the point format. Whether you are a beginner or have experience, this book will provide resources that will help you on your journey to internet success. I will go over a plethora of information such as: giving you actual business ideas to try, along with resource secrets and a host of other insightful points that will help set you on the right path. By the time you have finished reading this book, you will have the knowledge to empower yourself to go out and start making extra income online.

If you are reading this book, you probably already have an idea about why you would like to start an online business. Maybe you want to make a little extra money on the side. Maybe you wish to make enough money to someday quit your 9-5. Maybe you desire to have the flexibility to spend more time with family and friends doing things that you enjoy. Whatever your reasons, know them, embrace them, and keep them in the forefront of your mind at all times. As you journey through creating and maintaining your online business, you will find that focusing on your reasons for wanting an online business will keep you motivated to drive closer to your goals. This endeavor will have highs and lows. There may be days that you are pleasantly overwhelmed by a sea of new orders from your website, and other days where business is sluggish. No matter what scenario you find your self in, do not falter. Consistency, and persistency, are the keys to success. So get ready to flip the page and write down " Why do I want an online business?" Write all of your answers/ goals and keep it somewhere safe. If you ever need the motivation, pull it out, re-read it and re-inspire yourself.

WHY DO I WANT AN ONLINE BUSINESS?

_____

_____

_____

_____

_____

_____

_____

_____

_____

_____

_____

_____

_____

_____

_____

_____

Initially, I started my online businesses to provide for and sustain myself economically. As my businesses grew, I realized that I also loved the freedom that I had as an online entrepreneur. I have no boss to answer to. I wake up when I want, go out when I want, and do things at my own leisure. If I want to have lunch for 3.5 hours I can do it without worrying if I'll still have a job tomorrow. This freedom is why I keep going. I remember how it felt to ask someone for permission to do what I wanted to do with my own time. I loathed that feeling. I guess I've always been a bit of a rebel, but I finally found my cause.

I have become obsessed with embracing my own freedom, and I love that. It still amazing me sometimes that I can be out on any given evening eating dinner, and check my email on my phone, and see that I sold a few products or made some affiliate revenue. I recently vacationed in the Bahamas and the year before, I traveled to Maui, Hawaii. One of the best feelings about being on vacation while owning an online business is that I didn't have to ask a manager if I could go on vacation. I decided when, where, and how long …and that was that. I didn't dread coming back to "work" when the trips were over. While away on vacation, my websites were up and generating income.

Even though there are a lot of luxuries to owning an online business, it is a lot of hard work, and responsibility. You have to be strong enough to tell yourself what to do, and disciplined enough to complete tasks that need to be done.

I cannot tell you how many people I've met who never got their businesses off the grown. This is one of the biggest challenges. If you're reading this, I believe you have enough guts to succeed.

Ok, back on topic! The freedom I get from my online businesses is true wealth to me- more so than the actual act of making money. Being able to make my own choices while making a living for myself is success for me.

So, after you have written out your goals to "Why you want an online business?", it's probably best that you also define "What is success?" to you. Whatever it may be, don't be afraid, write it and remind yourself of it daily. I know it may sound a bit cliché, but reminding yourself about your goals and your reasons for wanting to be an online entrepreneur will help keep you focused. The longer you are focused on what you want, and why you want it, the more likely it is that your business will be a success. You have to believe it, even if no one else does.

WHAT IS SUCCESS (TO ME)?

CHAPTER 2
THE FEAR FACTOR AND HOW TO ENCOURAGE YOURSELF TO SUCCESS

Through my conversations with many aspiring small e-business owners, I have discovered that one of the most common barriers to starting and maintaining an online business is fear. Fear of the unknown, not knowing where to start or how to start can keep you from starting at all. We will address fear head on in this chapter, as straight forward as possible. Fear is a natural human emotion. We are all afraid at times, but fear is something that should be embraced and challenged. Just because you may be afraid to try something new, does not necessarily mean that you should succumb to that fear. I believe that fear exists to be challenged and then to ultimately be conquered.

For as long as I can remember, I have wanted to own my own website and sell things. Lack of knowledge on where to get started turned into a fear that kept me from getting started. I didn't know anything about website coding, or graphic design, or where to find wholesalers. My desire for success eventually outweighed the fear that held me back. In other words, I needed to make extra income more than I wanted to be afraid of things that I didn't understand. Eventually, I started my first business and found out that it wasn't as scary as I had once anticipated.

If you want to create a successful online business, fear is not an option. You can create anything you desire with the right knowledge combined with courage. This is the truth that many people will not tell you. It can be applied to just about any facet of life. The goal of this book is to give you that knowledge, so that you can create your own destiny. Even after you get over the initial humps of starting your business, there may be challenges that arise along the way, but you have to remain focused, and challenge those fears as they come. This will allow your business to survive and thrive.

You might be asking yourself…"ok, well how do I challenge fear?" The first step is to identify exactly what you are afraid of. If you can be honest enough with yourself to admit what you are afraid of, then you can seek out the knowledge to overcome that fear. It's as simple as that. For example, before I started one of my businesses, I was afraid because I did not know where or how to get wholesalers in order to sell the specific products that I wanted to sell. My mind was racing, and I didn't know where to start. I had to calm myself down and identify the fear. After that, I knew what I had to do. I had to figure out how to find these products, period. If I wanted to build this business, that was my solution. After several weeks of rigorous researching and some risk taking, I found my venders. The end result is that I resolved an issue and I am no longer afraid. I identified what I was afraid of, and then sought out the knowledge to debunk that fear. Simple as pie, right?

Now, it's your turn:

WHAT AM I AFRAID OF?
(KEEP IT REAL)

_____

_____

_____

_____

_____

_____

_____

_____

_____

_____

_____

_____

Ok, I know sometimes things are easier said than done. But you have to encourage yourself daily. You have to believe in yourself and your ability to succeed, even if no one else believes in you. You have to think positive thoughts daily about yourself and your goals. Above all, you have to tell yourself that you CAN do anything you desire if you have the proper knowledge to do it. If you don't have the knowledge, you have to encourage yourself to seek it out. You are accomplishing this right now by reading *Black Guide to Money: 101 Secret Ways to Make Money Online*. Kudos to you!

PS. If you need assistance with locating venders, check out Chapter 8. You can also visit www.blackguidetomoney.com for even more resources.

CHAPTER 3
LET'S GET STARTED!

It goes without saying that the economy has fallen on really hard times. With rising unemployment rates, a plummeting housing market and a host of countless financial disasters; financial stability is a negative trending topic. Whether you are employed, unemployed, or underemployed, everyone wants to know how to make extra income these days.

It doesn't matter if you're seeking a full time cash flow, or if you just want to make it easier to enjoy a better lifestyle, finding a profitable hobby or way to make money seems to be on everyone's mind.

Rather than head out into a distressed job market, many people are tapping into the business of making money online. People are taking advantage of this opportunity because ecommerce is virtually accessible to everyone. As long as you have an internet connection and a computer, you can start making real money using the World Wide Web. Some of the benefits of using the internet to make money include:

- being able to work from home

- saving gas money
- having extra time to spend with family and friends
- having extra time to traveling
- being able to enjoy a more flexible schedule
- having the option to make money with little to no physical effort

Although many online opportunities are legitimate, some are predatory and should be avoided.

Before I discuss what you can do to make money online, I should uncover certain pitfalls and traps that you may encounter. For example, let's say you stumble on a site that swears you can "make $4,500 a week – and do almost nothing". Hmm… So you're skeptical, but you keep reading and then you click.

You read through all of the convincing testimonials and scroll to the bottom of the page and then it hits you! You haven't found out anything about this opportunity, and in order to find out, you're going to have to pay for the "money making system". The great part is that it is only $99.95! Out of curiosity, you sign up and pay for the "deal of a lifetime." You think to yourself "It has to be legit because the deal features a money back guarantee, right?" Wrong!! You find out the hard way that this money back guarantee is only valid for a small period of time that has already expired.

It's obvious that this is a scenario that you should avoid. You can make money online and it shouldn't have to involve buying into someone else's mysterious system. With that said, let's discuss legitimate opportunities that are available for you to take advantage of online.

Three Different Ways

In order to be successful at generating revenue online, there are three key activities that you should be pursuing in order to create the most effective results. Those three activities are:

- Performing a service
- Selling goods
- Advertising or Affiliate Marketing

For the sake of argument, I'm also going to add a category called "personal endeavors". This category may closely resemble the previous mentioned categories at times, however I would like to separate this subject because I feel that this area is a bit more exotic and may no be a desirable fit for all audiences.

The most common and widely adopted method is "selling goods". Lots of people do this online for extra income and really enjoy it. It's also likely that you are familiar with the concept of performing services. This is where much of the term "freelancing" online is utilized. I will discuss these categories in depth a bit later.

What you might not fully understand is the concept of online advertising and affiliate marketing. This is the idea that in the expansive world of the internet, there are millions of products and services. It is often difficult for a consumer to find a website with so many choices. Advertising and affiliate marketing involves placing ads using keywords and other tools to help connect internet users with products and services. When you choose to do any kind of online advertising and affiliate marketing, you're helping a person or company to sell their products.

So, now that you know a little more, let's talk about the ways that you can make money online. There is a lot that you might be interested in and I'll try to be specific, but you should consider all information carefully. Only invest time and energy in projects that you feel comfortable and confident in.

CHAPTER 4
E-COMMERCE

E-commerce is big business these days and it's projected to grow immensely in the future. Essentially, e-commerce is the industry in which someone provides electronic commerce (hence the name e-commerce). In simple terms, this basically means selling products over the internet. If you are thinking about selling products online, there are many platforms through which you can set up a shop.

3rd Party Selling Platforms:

These companies allow you to have an outlet to sell your products by using their website and their pre-established customer bases.

Some Popular 3rd Party Selling Platforms are :

eBay
Etsy
Craigslist
ArtFire
Facebook Marketplace

Now, I'll explain the pros and cons for each of the above.

eBay: an online user driven website for buying and selling goods.

Pros and Cons

Pros:
- Instant access to thousands of potential customers
- Low user fees based on your individual business' sales, and you don't have to pay most fees upfront. Most fees are due once a month, typically at the beginning of the new month.
- Users might feel safer purchasing from an already known website with trusted security and buyer protection (eBay uses PayPal which offers its customers protection against faulty products).

Cons:
- High competition. If you aren't selling something completely unique, it may be hard for customers to find you amongst the masses. Sometimes high competition also means settling for a lower price. If you're selling an item that a customer can purchase

from several other eBay sellers what will make them choose you? Often times, sellers might aim for lower prices in the hopes to get more sales. This might be ok if you're getting enough sales to make a decent profit margin.

- Difficulty branding. If you are trying to go big and create your own brand, chances are you will eventually outgrow eBay. It's hard to create a reputable brand if you don't have your own .com.

- The occasional dishonest customer. Sometimes customers bid on items and never pay once they win. Other times buyers may abuse the buyer protection. On rare occasions, a customer might buy an item and claim that they never received it, in the hopes to file a dispute, so that they can get their money back (which basically means they're trying to get a free product). Safety notes: adding "Signature Confirmation" to packages verifies that the customer actually received the product because they have to sign for it. In addition, always ship to "confirmed" PayPal addresses. Confirmed addresses are verified by PayPal to be the authentic address of the buyer.

My experience with eBay success

Use eBay for what it's worth. Sell to your little heart's content. Long before I ever owned any websites, I sold my first products through eBay. It's a great platform to build a trusty customer base and make extra money. Also, some sellers become power houses and make hundreds of thousands of dollars from eBay sales. Try to offer niche items, that are harder for competing sellers to source and provide. This may make you stand out, which could increase your chances for frequent sales. Test out the "Buy it Now" feature vs the "Auction" feature and see which avenue brings you the most success. In my past eBay experience, I had most of my sales success by using the classic auction function. I think that customers become enticed to participate in "bidding wars". There is something alluring about seeing the clock count down while battling against other users to win an auction.

Etsy: an online user generated marketplace for buying and selling handmade goods, vintage items and art supplies.

Pros and Cons

Pros:
-   Instant access to thousands of potential customers
-   Cheap listing fees. Etsy only charges 20 cents to list an item on their site. You can't beat that.
-   A neat interactive social media platform for all your products. Meaning, people can "tweet", "like" and now "pin" your products to sites like Twitter, Facebook and Pinterest.
-   Every user has the free option to create a "store", with a personalized url.

Cons:
-   Not as much traffic as eBay
-   Buyers often use Etsy as a social media platform admiring the items vs actually buying them. For example, products you list on Etsy can be "admired" and added to "treasury lists" by other users. While it might make you smile that you have 350 people admiring your handmade earrings, what you really

want them to do is to click the "Add to Cart" button to solidify it.
- Handcrafted items can sometimes be time consuming and are limited by how much you can make. Meaning, you can only sell what you produce.

My opinions for Etsy success

Use Etsy to compliment your hustle. If you sell handmade soap through artist markets, co-workers or family members, why not toss them on your Etsy store and broaden your market? If you also blog or use Facebook to talk about your crafty products, having a formal Etsy store can help you generate more sales. Think big!

Craigslist: an online free classifieds connection place.

Pros and Cons

Pros:
- Can be a great option for selling expensive goods like: cars, houses, furniture and high end jewelry.
- Instant gratification. If you conduct "cash only" sales, once the sale is finalized you get your money and the customer gets their product and you're both good to go.
- Access to all Craigslist users, which gives your advertisement instant traffic.
- Free 99! Craigslist is free and everybody knows you can't beat free.

Cons:

- Great for starters, but not the most visually aesthetic way to advertise. The truth is some people don't shop on Craigslist because they don't think it's a legitimate website.
- Spammers. Craigslist has a major spamming issue, and sometimes it may be frustrating for potential customers to sift through all the junk in order to find your ad.
- Scammers. There are a lot of scam artist on Craigslist, but once you know what to look for it's easy to spot them. If someone gives you a long story about how they live overseas and they want you to wire them money to another country… chances are it's a scam. Stay away from personal checks and cashier checks- they can easily be fraudulent. Similarly, if someone asks for your PayPal account email, run the other way (unless you can google them to see if they're a real person). The PayPal email scam generally works like this: once you give your email out, they'll eventually send you an official-looking email that appears to be sent from PayPal. Once you click it, you either get a virus or you'll get a pop-up of a fake website that looks exactly like PayPal, asking you to login. If you enter your login information on the fake site, the scammer now has access to your PayPal account.

My opinions for Craigslist success

Craigslist is the perfect hustling grounds for shameless promoters. If you would like to post ads on Craigslist, refresh your posting every few days so that it still appears new and relevant. Note: there's a thin line between doing this and spamming people with tons of duplicate postings every single day. I've used CL for selling high-end jewelry in the past and had really good luck with it. Always be safe when meeting up with people to exchange goods. Agree to meet in the day-time in public places: malls, police stations, banks, etc. Consider meeting places that correspond with the item that you're selling. For example, if you're selling a car, agreeing to meet at a mechanic's shop can help the buyer feel confident in the car's analysis, which can possibly lead to a sale.

Artfire: an online membership art website for buying and selling fine art, vintage items and handmade goods.

Pros and Cons

Pros:
- Instant access to thousands of potential customers
- Free 14 day trial and then $12.95 per month flat rate, with no additional fees.

Cons:
- Lower traffic than eBay and Etsy. A lot of people aren't familiar Artfire because it's still pretty new. This could mean fewer and less frequent sales.

My opinions for Artfire success

Artfire may be great for beginners or for someone who is trying to get that Etsy-like audience but with fewer fees. It might also work well for sellers that have a lot of inventory, because their flat rate seller plan gives you unlimited selling potential with the least amount of fees. I'd say, there's no harm in giving it a try and seeing if it will work out for you. Sometimes business is about trial and error, or trial and success. If you are a well know artist in your community and have a pre-existing customer base, Artfire maybe a great platform to direct your customers and followers to purchase your work.

Facebook Marketplace: Facebook's online classified ad outlet (similar to Craigslist).

Pros and Cons

Pros:
- Sharing information about your products with friends and family with just a few simple clicks.
- The ability to sell products to people who aren't your friends or family members, but who are also Facebook users
- Yep... it's free!

Cons:
- Sometimes the marketplace can appear to be a little spammy.
- Lacks confidentiality / true privacy. Unlike Craigslist, Facebook Marketplace will show other users your profile picture and name, along with the item(s) you are selling. They also occasionally send emails announcing what items you're selling to users who are your friends. They do allow you the ability to narrow down specific groups of friends who can see your products (family, co-workers, classmates). This may make some users feel a bit uneasy.

My opinions for Facebook Marketplace success

Facebook Marketplace can be a good tool for spreading the word about your business by promoting the products that you're trying to sell. If you are skeptical about the lack of privacy, you should consider creating a Facebook business page instead of using your personal page. People see your business name and business information instead of your personal details. Business pages are free, and allow other FB users the option to "Like" your company's page.

Free Websites

I have received several questions about this topic, and I have to keep it real with my readers. So... brace yourself.

What are "free" websites?

Free websites are essentially websites that are hosted through a parent website. The parent website is an "umbrella" to anyone who is looking to create a store by using the parent company's name. These sites might allow you to have a free a customizable url, but in most instances you are not getting a free genuine *yourcompany.com* domain name type of deal. In many instances your domain name will look something like this:
Yourcompany.webs.com or *yourcompany.yolasite.com*.

To be honest, I've never been a fan of these types of sites and I'll tell you why in just a second. But first, to be fair, I'll list several popular free sites below just to make sure you are aware of your options.

Yola
Weebly
Webs
Ecrater
Wix

For the sake of practicality, I'm going to combine these sites into one group because most of them tend to share similar pros and cons.

Pros
- Easy-to-use interfaces that don't require a lot of coding experience
- Quick set-up. You can have a store set up in a matter of minutes.
- Free customizable urls (as described above)
- PayPal integration. Most free sites offer PayPal shopping carts so you can easily get paid by customers.
- Premium paid membership options (which might include paying an extra fee to have an authentic .com domain name).

Cons (here it goes guys, I said I was going to keep it real)

- Bad Search Engine Optimization (SEO). SEO is essentially your visibility power on the net. It's what helps people find you when they're on search engines like Google or Yahoo. In Most cases, free sites don't have the best SEO and if people can't find you, then they can't buy your products.

- A lot of free sites have advertisements on them, letting anyone who visits your site know that your website was created free.
- Ridiculously long and hard to remember urls. Let's be honest, a lot of people are lazy and won't take the extra time to enter your extra long domain name. Made-up Example: *www.Kikisclothingshop.yolasite.com*... really?? Who's going to take the time to remember and enter this kind of address on more than one occasion? Chances are, no one.
- Low traffic equals little or no sales.

My honest opinion about "free" websites

When are "free sites" a good idea?
- When you are not using them with an expectation to sell products. Such as, using a free site to simply display a general profile about you or your business.
- When you already have a very strong pre-existing customer base that is willing to follow your business to a free site.
- When you pay for one of their premium services – thus, making your website non-free (such as registering a genuine .com domain name and not having spammy advertisements).

My Conclusion About Free Sites:

Don't take the easy way out. People create these sites in a few minutes and then wonder why they're not getting many or any sales. In most cases, these free sites are not generating good organic traffic. I would recommend staying away from them. For the most part, free websites show that you are a beginner and are essentially the equivalent to receiving a business card with "this card was printed for free with Vistaprint" on the back. People won't say it to your face, but most will not take your business seriously. Success has no short cuts. If you would like to have a income generating website, spend an extra $10 bucks or so, and purchase a true domain name. It shows that you are thorough and serious enough about your business to invest in it.

Paid Websites With All-in-one Shopping Cart Software

These platforms are a few of my favorite resources for creating your website. How do they work? Essentially, you pay a monthly fee and you have your very own .com website with a fully integrated shopping cart.

A Few Paid Shopping Cart Solutions
Volusion
Shopify
3dCart

Again, for the sake of practicality, I will lump all of these paid cart solutions into one group. They're birds of a feather. If you think this might be a good choice for you, research these companies and go with the one that best fits your individual business needs.

Pros and Cons

Pros:
- All inclusive. Most paid cart solutions offer a variation of services including your: domain name, hosting, website template choices and a shopping cart. The fact that you can get everything you need from one place is a major selling point.
- Monthly plans that cater to your specific product count and or your monthly bandwidth. Bandwidth measures the amount of visits your website gets. If your site is just starting off, lower bandwidth means a cheaper plan. As your store grows, you can always adjust your plans to reflect the business.
- Built in accounting platforms that help you keep track of your monthly sales
- Stylish modern website template designs options
- Easy-to-use. No major coding experience required
- Better search engine visibility, which means that it may be easier for people to find your business when browsing the web

Cons:
- Plans can be a little costly. If your business is not getting a lot of sales, the month to month fees can really add up over time.

My opinions for paid shopping cart success

This is an all around great choice. As you see, I did not have a lot of cons to list here. If you are going to invest in a paid shopping cart solution, I would advise you to invest time and money into marketing your business. It doesn't have to cost a lot, but you want to make sure that people are visiting the site that you're paying for. Consider paying for digital advertisement through Google Adwords. You get to pick how much or little you want to spend for ads (as long as it's more than $10). I have used Adwords for a little over 4 years and the ads keep a steady flow of traffic visiting my websites. More traffic equals more sales. Make sure that you are utilizing social media platforms like Twitter, YouTube, and Facebook. You might also want to consider traditional forms of advertisement or grass roots in your face marketing. Whatever your choices, be consistent. Advertising is not just a one time thing. It's "branding" your company. You consistently want to remind people that your business is open, and that they are welcomed to click on over and shop.

Free (Open-Source) Shopping Cart Platforms

What are they?
Free shopping cart platforms offer complimentary software to it's users. This free software is sometimes referred to as "open-source" because it openly allows users the freedom to use and share the software at no cost. Now let's be clear, open-source does not really mean that you get a completely free website. You only get a free shopping cart platform, which allows your website to look and function like a true online store. You still have to pay for and register your domain name (yourstore.com) and you still have to pay for

website hosting. Hosting allows your website to be visible on the web.

Here are a few free shopping cart choices:

VirtueMart
Magento
OsCommerce
PrestaShop
Zen Cart

Pros and Cons

Pros
- One less thing to pay for!
- Highly customizable. If you have any coding skills, you can customize templates to compliment your store's shopping cart experience.
- Stylish template options
- Ease of use. There may be an initial learning curve, but if you practice you can get the hang of it.

Cons
- Sometimes free carts are more prone to having glitches / bugs.
- Potential lack of customer support , if you have an issue with your shopping cart.

My opinion:

Free carts are an awesome choice for those looking for an economically savvy way to have a legitimate looking website. If you don't have any coding experience, consider purchasing a low cost pre-made website template that utilizes the cart software. You can purchase predesigned templates at TemplateMonster.com. I would also suggest occasionally (at least once a year, if not more) contracting a web programmer to check your website and perform updates to it. This will help ensure that your website is performing as it should.

CHAPTER 5
SERVICE-BASED BUSINESSES

A service-based business will allow you to get paid to perform a particular service that you specialize in. There are two different ways that you can make money online by having a service-based business.

The first way is to freelance your skills strictly through the internet. Freelancing is a way of contracting your services out for a short time period to a client for a fee. This method allows you to perform your services from the comfort of your home or anywhere else that you wish. These services are most likely transacted digitally. For example, digital freelancing can include: graphic designing, website coding, photography submissions, blogging, or just about anything else that you can deliver by e-mail. One of my favorite secret resources for making money by freelancing is Elance.com. You can sign up for free and get hired to work as a contractor for companies looking to hire individuals with your specialty.

The second way to make money online for services, is to market a service online that you would perform in person.

So, if you are a lawn care professional, you could use the internet to market to clients to get sales. If you are a hairstylist or barber, you might want to take advantage of internet marketing as well as digitally booking clients. Schedulicity.com is an awesome booking software that could help make your brick and mortar business more successful.

Ideas for skillful artists:
If you are a creative person with lots of artistic talent, consider marketing your skills on Craiglist. If you are a dj, apply to dj gigs. If you are a photographer, post up ads with your pricing and let the world know you are available for hire. Use the internet to help you grow your business! We're living in the technology era and there's no reason to leave money on the table. Think bigger!

WHAT SKILLS DO I HAVE THAT I CAN TAKE TO THE WEB?

_____

_____

_____

_____

_____

_____

_____

_____

_____

_____

_____

_____

_____

CHAPTER 6
MAKING MONEY FROM ADVERTISING, AFFILIATE MARKETING, AND REFERRAL MARKETING

One of the most automated ways to make money online is by advertising and affiliate marketing. In this chapter, I will discuss different ways that you can take advantage of these opportunities. First, let me say that this is one of my favorite methods for making money online. Advertising and Affiliate market doesn't involve the hassles of shipping physical products or interacting with customers. It's an easy way to create passive income for your bank account.

Before I get ahead of myself, I will define what these techniques are how you can start taking advantage of them.

What is online advertising?

Online advertising is essentially the system of advertising on the internet. It generally involves a two fold process. Let's say someone is looking to promote their business on the web, so they might sign up to an advertising program like Google's Adwords. In this program, they pay a fee to Google to display their business' banners all over the internet. The second part of this process is that there are other people out here who are called publishers. Publishers allow those advertisements to be visible on their website.

The later part of the advertising process mentioned above is the specific type of advertising that I'm referring to in this chapter. It is formally called Pay Per Click (PPC) or Cost Per Click (CPC). The PPC is the amount of money you earn each time a user "clicks" on the ads displayed on your website.

How to become an ad publisher

First, you have to sign up for an account with a program that pays publishers. I highly recommend Google Adsense. Setting up an Adsense account is totally free and only takes a few minutes to do.
Once you've signed up, you can display ads by using these easy steps below:

1. Log into your Google Adsense account.
2. At the top of your login page click on the tab that reads "My ads".
3. On the new page click "New ad unit".
4. This will take you to an area where you can customize the way you would like the advertisement to appear on your website. For example, you can choose an ad size, color, whether or not you want text only or picture ads, etc.
5. After you've selected the visual details of the ads, click the button at the bottom of the page that reads "Save and get code".
6. You should now see an html code that appears (if you've never seen html before, it will look like a bunch of gibberish). You will need to put this code on your website. If you do not know how to do this, you can always hire a freelance coder off of Elance.com for around $5-10 bucks.

7. The ad should be visible on your website typically within 30 minutes or less. Note: you'll have to repeat these steps for each different type of ad that you want displayed on your site.

How to get paid for displaying ads

Using the PPC system, Google monitors how many different people click on the advertisements that are displayed on your website. Each click generates a certain amount of revenue based off of what the original advertiser has specified. The more visits your website gets, the more clicks you will get. After you have generated at least $100 in ad revenue, Google will disperse the funds to your bank account or whatever payment method you request.

My personal tips on how to get paid for being a publisher

You might be thinking that just because you have advertisements on your website, you are going to make a ton of money. This is far from the truth. There is definitely a formula for success for people looking to make money through ads. The formula is high traffic = more money. Over the past several years, I've owned a little over 20 websites and I know first hand that I've made the most money off of the websites that have a higher traffic flow. I recommend making sure you promote your website as best as you can to ensure you have a lot of people visiting it. If you aren't getting a lot of visits to your website, chances are you aren't really going to make money off of the ads. You also need to remember that if you don't make at least $100 you will not get paid. Google does not disperse funds until you have generated at least this amount of money.

Affiliate Marketing

Affiliate marking is another easy way to make money online. It's very similar to how Google Adsense works but slightly different. With affiliate marketing, you sign up to be an "affiliate" for a specific company (sometimes these companies are also referred to as "merchants"). Once you've signed up, you are supplied with an html code that allows you to incorporate a company's advertisement banner on your website. With affiliate marketing, you get paid a commission when someone clicks on the advertisement and actually buys a product or service. So, lets say you sign up to be an affiliate for a company that sells shoes. Usually, in order for you to get paid, the person who clicks on the shoe advertisement will actually have to purchase a pair of shoes from the merchants website.

Some cool affiliate marketing companies to check out:

Amazon.com
ClickBank.com
CampusBookRentals.com
NetFlix.com
KarmaLoop.com
Sittercity.com

Affiliate Networks

If you think you might have a hard time looking for different affiliates to choose from, you might want to consider signing up to an affiliate network. Affiliate networks are websites that market multiple merchants. You can browse through and sign up to be an affiliate to several different companies all at the same time. ShareASale.com is a great affiliate network to check out. Google also has an awesome affiliate network program.

Referral Marketing

Sometimes companies want you to display their advertisements on your website because they are looking to pay you for the leads that you are able to you generate for them. Leads are people who express interest in a product or service (future potential customers). This is called referral marketing and you can sign up to "referral programs" in order to take advantage of this online opportunity. Some people also call this type of marketing Pay Per Lead (PPL).

How it works:

First, sign up with a PPL company and place their advertisement on your website. You can find PPL programs on *ShareASale.com*. Referral programs will usually require some type of information from the leads who click on the advertisement in order to pay you for promoting their company. Sometimes this information can be simply joining an email list, other times, referral programs may ask potential customers to fill out a survey to decide whether or not each person is a real candidate for their products or services. On occasions, people use the terms "referral programs" and "affiliate programs" interchangeably, but remember the difference is that affiliate programs almost always require actual sales to take place.

CHAPTER 7

PERSONAL ENDEVORS

Making money online from your own personal endeavors can be defined as pursuing any business venture that is reflective of your own lifestyle and personality. For example, if you love to act consider offering acting classes on Craigslist or your own website. Leverage your time online with your hobbies and things that you love to do. The last chapter of this book will give you more examples to consider.

CHAPTER 8

101 WAYS TO MAKE MONEY ONLINE

Now that I've given you all of this fabulous information, it's time to jump into the 101 secret ways to make money online! If you're looking to succeed online it takes a lot of effort and consistency. I encourage you to conduct additional research to help you make the best choices for yourself and your business. Log on to our website at www.BlackGuidetoMoney.com for additional tips and resources.

101 Ways to Make Money Online:

Selling Products

1. **Sell jewelry online.** Nowadays, jewelry is a really hot topic. Consider purchasing jewelry for wholesale prices and reselling it on your website. Because jewelry is a low cost item, profit margins are usually pretty attractive. Make sure you promote your products as much as possible, because you will probably need to sell a lot of pieces in order to collect a larger sum of money. Check out *wholesalejewelry.net* and *jewelrymax.net*

2. **Use eBay to sell things that you already own.** Sell household items that you never use on eBay or a similar site. You should look for similar items to see what they go for – this will help you to decide what you should ask for your things.

3. **Consider selling accessories like sunglasses or handbags.** You might want to try your hand at selling these items online. There might be a little investment when you do this, but if you can get consistent sales, it may prove to be worthwhile. If you're going to go this route visit *Huafu.org*

4. **Flip websites.** This process does take a little bit of money for start up, but all you really have to do is buy a domain name and then resell it for more money. It might be a slow start at first, but with a little time, you'll find that you can make some decent money by doing it. Visit *Sedo.com*

5. **Write and sell your own eBook.** You'll find them all over online, but if you have something to say and can write about it in the proper format, you might have a

winning product. You can combine this with another project such as your gardening website, or you can go it alone. Remember, the key here is to get your product noticed.

6. **Hand make products and sell them through your website or Etsy.com** If you have a great product idea, you might want to sell it online. All you need is a website which you can get rather inexpensively. If you want to set yourself apart from the crowd, try to offer items that are unique as possible.

7. **Start up an online store that focuses on the environment.** The environment is a big deal these days and you can make a decent income from selling products that are cost effective and easy to use for those who are looking for ways to offset their carbon footprint. You can sell everything from books, to fashionable eco-friendly clothing to Earth friendly skin care products.

8. **Sell phone cases and related accessories online.** The cell-phone accessory business is a multi-billion dollar industry. Although there is a lot of competition, you might still be able to get your slice of the pie. Check out *Reikowireless.com*

9. **Sell pre-made web pages.** Even when you freelance your web skills, you might still want to offer different web page layouts that people can buy for a smaller fee than what you charge to make custom pages. When you make them fully customizable, you might find that you can compete with bigger companies that offer web sites to choose from.

10. **Sell products under a pre-existing company's website.** Companies such as Mary Kay, Scentsy, and Avon just to name a few have given their sales consultants more freedom by offering them websites.

You might find that this is a great way to make extra money and you don't have to leave your home to do it. The trick is in the promotion.

Performing a Service

11. **Freelance your skills building websites.** Do you know how to build top notch websites? You might find that you can make a really great living by offering your services on a freelance basis. Establish a good portfolio and build a client list. Visit *csstemplatesweb.com*

12. **Write – and submit your work to article directories.** If you're a good writer, you can make a little extra by writing for article directories. This might not be a great income, but you can make a little extra and when you do a little networking, the byline could be really helpful for you.

13. **Freelance write for print or ezines.** Take it a step further and consider freelance writing for magazines. The competition is pretty fierce, but if you have some great ideas and have a strong writing background, you might find that many magazines want to buy your work. You can get most of your contact information online and in some cases; you will even find magazines that are seeking writers.

14. **Freelance as a graphic artist.** If you've got an artistic hand you might want to consider becoming a freelance graphic artist. You might only do these as side jobs, but every little bit extra can help. Many freelance graphic artists will use freelance sites to start up a client list and get their business going. Visit *graphicriver.net*

15. **Work as a virtual assistant.** If you have killer office and communication skills, you might be perfect to become a virtual assistant. Often with a position such as this, you will be paid as an independent contractor, which means that your employer does not pay your taxes or offer benefits, but you will have a set schedule and receive and hourly wage.

16. **Use your skills to help businesses get more traffic to their sites.** Help some of your local businesses get more business by developing a web presence for them. Many business owners don't have the time or knowledge to get the website traffic that they need, but you can help. If you're familiar with SEO writing and know a little bit about the way common search engines work, you can help many small businesses and make money in the process.

17. **Install Upgrades and Plugins for WordPress.** If you know WordPress, you can install plugins and upgrades. Since there is such a demand for this, you can really make a good living at it. Some people will charge around $5 a plugin and it will only take a few minutes to do. Consider working off a site that offers contractors for this sort of thing and you might find that you're making a decent amount of money.

18. **Use social media sites to make money.** Small businesses and bloggers could use your help by submitting their blog posts or websites to some of your social media websites. You know Facebook and you probably spend time on it, so why not make money with the time you spend there? It's pretty dull, but you can make some money doing it.

19. **Start up a website for a special niche.** Say you love to garden. You love the idea of organic gardening even more, but you know that many people don't

know how. You can get your special niche out there and the advertisements that you put on your site will help you to make money with it.

20. **If you have information that people want, start a membership site for people to join.** You've seen some of them, such as Angie's List that offers all the information you need about contractors for many projects and other types of sites. The key is for you to have a vast knowledge about something that others want to know. This takes research, but can be very rewarding. In the case of contractors that might benefit, you can probably charge them a small fee to be featured.

21. **Take great products you find offline and market them online.** Whether it's that fabulous jam that the local fruit lady makes, or it's something else, most of the time, the owners of these products will be willing to talk turkey when it comes to you promoting them online. Do your homework and have a good plan before you start for best results.

22. **Think about travel writing.** This is another type of freelance work that might appeal to you if you're well traveled. A good way to make your mark is to be aware of great bargain travel deals out there and be able to reveal the pros and cons of each destination to readers.

23. **Do other people's research.** You can get new clients online and if you're good at it, you could make lots – and lots of money at it. These days, you don't always have to make a trip the library because you can do it all from your home computer and that makes your work even more profitable. Visit *odesk.com*

24. **Start an online tutoring service.** With Skype and other ways to virtually connect, this can be an easy

and cost effective way to not only be a tutor, but make some extra money. Get prospective clients through your local schools and be ready to show your credentials and be sure to offer your email address.

25. **Test video games.** If you're a gamer, then you're going to love this option. Consider checking with Microsoft or some of the other game companies and finding out if you might qualify for this type of money making opportunity.

26. **Write SEO articles.** If you know anything about Google and ranking a website, you know that it all lies in proper search engine optimization. The rules have changed recently though, so if you know the new rules, you're likely to rack up some big business. The great news is that there are lots of new website owners who are seeking this service, so it might be great for you to do. Visit *freelancer.com*

27. **Become a blogger - for yourself or someone else.** Whenever you start blogging, you should have your own blog. Even if it's small, it's going to go a long way in helping you to get the high paying blogging gigs that you're seeking. Check out *Elance.com*

28. **Create a website where you rank local businesses and entertainment.** It might have been done already, but in many areas, the more free or inexpensive advertisements a company can get, the happier they are. You can make it a membership site and put new money saving offers up every week or so.

29. **Make and sell personalized WordPress themes.** WordPress is a very big deal these days and while many people have a pretty basic understanding of it, they don't know how to do all the really great things that can be done with this common website writing tool. That's where you come in. If you can design it,

you can make big money creating customized themes for others. Visit *ThemeForest.net*

30. **Start creating smart phone apps.** If you've ever looked at your smart phone and thought that it would be so cool to have that app, or thought you could make an app better, then you might want to start doing this for a living. It can be a little tricky and you'll have to have an understanding, but once you get going, you can really make a great living doing this.

31. **Become an Event Coordinator.** Love planning parties and events?, consider expanding your services online. The key is to start small locally and pay attention to what businesses and non-profit agencies are looking for in their events. If you can minimize event expenses and maximize the amount of money they will bring in for their event, then you'll have a place in this industry. Consider listing events on *eventbrite.com*

32. **Create a free referral website.** You make your money by signing up your chosen service providers. Your job is to do the background checks, etc and charge a fee for contractors to be listed on your site. When they book a job through your site, you get a percentage of their earnings. You'll draw more individuals seeking services because it will be free for them.

33. **Start a store in a virtual world.** You've probably heard about this and if you are part of a virtual world, you can potentially make some decent money doing this. Just like people need things in the real world, they need things in their virtual worlds, so if you get the right niche, you can really make good money.

34. **Become an independent contractor for a company.** Many companies are seeking people to do

almost everything – from working a call center to preparing simple documents from home. If you're an independent contractor, you're going to have a schedule, but will be responsible for your own taxes and benefits.

35. **Enter data online.** You have to be careful with this sort of money making project, but there are some legitimate companies that do want you to simply enter data for them. If you find the right company, you might make some money doing this. Lots of people perform work on Facebook through *CloudCrowd.com.*

36. **Become a medical transcriptionist.** With the costs of insurance and expenses to health care professionals these days, the number of office staff is declining. This might mean that you have a great opening. You'll have to get the education to make this happen, but most of the time; you can do this job and submit it online to your doctor's clients.

37. **Do homework for students that are lazy.** Answer common questions for money and watch your account rack up some money. It's not going to make you rich, but you can definitely make some fun money with this type of extra. You can get started at *studentoffortune.com* and *notehall.com*

38. **Get paid to give your opinion on new websites.** Companies need your input and this is the way that you can make sure you are heard. You won't make a whole lot of money doing it, but if you have a little bit of time, you'll find that you can make a little bit of fun money.

39. **Take and sell stock photos.** Love taking pictures? You know, of flowers, trees, sunsets – anything really. You can sell those photos as stock photos. Check out getting started at *Fotolia.com* or a similar site. It might

take a lot of sales to actually support yourself, but you might really be surprised at how far this takes you.

40. **Become media relations pro.** If you're able to share good news with enthusiasm and are pretty good at damage control, you might love this type of position. You can freelance your skills and have more than one client, but you need to be available and able to get out to the media when necessary.

41. **Write and sell documents.** Not just any types of documents though, because these are for people that know how to write contracts, investor directories and that sort of thing. It's not for everyone, but if you know how to prepare legal documents, you're might find this works for you. Check out *Gazhoo.com* to get started.

42. **Become an online consultant.** You set yourself up as an expert on anything you choose, decide on your fees and get an internet phone number. You make money. It's a little bit like doing online counseling for money. Check out Ether.com and you might get started.

43. **Freelance any of your skills.** Whether you want to babysit, walk dogs or clean houses, there is a way to get the work you want on a per project basis. Find a generic freelance website like *PeoplePerHour.com* and get started working your way today.

44. **Test software for companies.** If you know about computers and software then you might want to consider working on a team of software testers and quality assurance people. You'll help to eliminate bugs of many types of software and you might find you really enjoy it.

45. **Clean up the internet.** If you have free time on your hands, then you might want to check this out. You go

through sites and look for the illicit stuff that's out there and get paid for it. Great way to make money, so check out *CrowdFlower.com.*

46. **Become an online accountant.** Guess what? If you're an out of work accountant or are just looking for some extra work, then you're in luck because lots of start-up companies are looking for good online accountants. This is a great way to freelance because you're likely to land ongoing clients.

47. **Make logos for small companies.** You might not make a killing doing this, but you're helping small businesses. You can use a program that helps you design logos and still make money when you sign up with a site like *Brandstack.com.*

48. **Start a web hosting business.** You'll need to learn a little if you're not familiar with the process, but once you get started, this can be a really great way to make some money. You have to handle the maintenance, but you'll also reap rewards from being a competitive smaller hosting business.

49. **Write grant proposals for non-profits or other businesses/schools/sports teams, etc.** Money is tight all around, so when you learn how to write grant proposals, you might find some pretty big money. Remember you charge according to how good you are, but if you charge a flat rate per hour and a certain percentage of the final reward; you can make a decent income doing this.

50. **Ghost-write eBooks for people.** This falls under freelance writing, but it's a pretty specific niche. To do this and do it well, you're going to need to know a little bit about the formatting of eBooks and how to make them more attractive to buyers. Here's a hint: it's really pretty easy. Once you know that, you can

help the millions out there that don't know how to do it – and get paid.

51. **Become a web analytics professional**. This falls under freelance, but with a tough economy like this one, you're going to find that your expertise can be really helpful. You'll explore how long people look at your client's site, if they make a purchase and how likely people are to stick around when they visit.

52. **Help people market their eBooks.** This is a bit trickier, but if you know about the way to market products online and SEO writing, you can use article directories to help promote these eBooks and make some really great sales. You can offer it as a package or you can charge by the article.

53. **Consider online juries.** Yes, you can be a part of this. Lots of lawyers need practice and this is where you can help them. You sign up and if you're selected, you get to be part of a mock trial. Stay involved and interested and you'll find that you get called back often. Check out *www.ejury.com* or *www.trialjuries.com* to get started.

54. **Mechanical Turk from Amazon can help.** This is a place where you can go to do simple tasks throughout your day to make money. It's not a whole lot of pay, but it can definitely add up, so check out some of the simple things you can do here. *www.mturk.com*

55. **If you know how to transcribe interviews, you can transcribe audio.** Market your services through a site like *www.edesk.ie* and if you can hear well and are a native English speaker with a strong understanding of the language, you might find you're making money in no time.

56. **Become a financial analyst or forecaster.** You'll help businesses to stay on top of trends to prepare for

the good – and bad times. As an online financial specialist, you'll be a number cruncher, but you already know how to do this. Sign up with a freelance site and get the clients you want and you'll both see your business grow.

57. **Online tax consultants and preparers freelance too.** You can freelance your skills as a licensed tax preparer or consultant. Many new businesses are seeking an online tax consultant to help them decide how to get the tax breaks they seek and make sure their taxes are in line and this is where you come in.

58. **If you know software, become an expert and help others.** If clients are having trouble installing anything from QuickBooks to Plesk Billing, did you know that people will pay you big bucks to help them install it? You just have to be really good at it, so show off your skill and make money for it at the same time.

59. **Write weekly or monthly newsletters for companies.** This might require that you are knowledgeable about the internal events of the companies you're working for, but once you have a few ongoing clients, this can make you a decent amount of money.

60. **Consider becoming a freelance copywriter or copyeditor.** If you're good at this, you're going to find that everything you do turns to gold for your client and you'll have more repeat work than you know what to do with. What's even better is the hourly rate that you can charge with this work. Plus, you won't even need to leave your home. Visit *www.demandstudios.com*

61. **Become a freelance online attorney.** Most of the time, the work is relatively simple, you prepare

documents such as non-disclosure agreements and contracts, but the pay is great and you're using your education to the fullest. Whether you're out of work or supplementing, you might find you enjoy the clients you have. Visit *www.hireanesquire.com*

62. **Produce videos that help to market companies.** Lots of businesses are seeking videos to explain products and make an impact in the world. If you can produce great ones, you're going to find that this is a career you can hold onto for a long time.

63. **Become an ad specialist.** If you know about advertising you can tie this into the online world for clients looking to build a solid online presence. When you do this freelance, you might find that lots of businesses enlist your help.

64. **Focus on ecommerce.** If you're an ecommerce specialist, you'll help businesses that are starting out to become ready for business. Your knowledge with Pay Pal setup and credit card payment systems will not only make you some great money, but you'll help your clients to be organized and ready for business.

65. **Become an online translator.** If you speak two or more languages, your skills are in demand. From small documents that need to be translated, to the longer textbook types of writings, you will find that this is a freelancing niche that can help you earn a really good income. Visit *www.proz.com*

66. **Be a human resources consultant.** When you freelance your human resources background, you're going to find that lots of businesses need your expertise. You'll find that you often help to draft policies for the work place and organize other policies that businesses need to maintain an employee – employer friendly environment.

67. **Surf the internet and get paid.** This won't make you rich, but if you spend a lot of time just cruising around online, you're likely to like this type of opportunity. You should only use sites that you trust though, because you can get scammed with this type of work. Check out Cash Crate to find out more.

68. **Share your files and make money.** Check out some sites that will allow you to upload almost any type of file and make money every single time someone downloads it. This is a great way to make some money off things like stories, photos and more. *Depositfiles.com* and *docstock.com* are great places to start.

69. **Become a legitimate mystery shopper.** There has been a lot of controversy about this type of making money and you will likely have to visit places in your area to make money, but once you're done and submit a report, you can make money for your shopping trips. Some reputable companies include *Beyondhello.com* and *www.a-closer-look.com.*

70. **If you're creative make designs for everything from t-shirts to coffee mugs.** You can flex your creative muscle by making up fun catch phrases and logos for customizable products that people buy. Consider a site like *spreadshirt.com* or etsy.com to get started.

71. **Directory submission might work well.** If you've got time, you should consider submitting websites to directories and get paid for it. This is how many sites generate traffic, but webmasters don't have the time to do it. You can check out sites like *DigitalPoint.com* or *SitePoint.com* to get going.

72. **What can you do for $5?** You can find out on *Fiverr.com.* This is the site where you can go and do just about anything for $5. If you can do it for five

bucks, you can make money and do it quickly. You might be surprised at how easy it is.

73. **Refer people for jobs – and get paid.** Did you know that there are actually companies that will pay you up to $1000 for a solid referral to fill a position? You can make that money when you can find the right people for the job. If you know recruiters and temp services, or can develop a network with them, you can refer people that you know will be great for the positions that are out there.

74. **Socialize and make money.** There are lots of new startup social networking sites out there that would love to become big, but they need members. This is where you come in because they will pay you to become a member, make friends online and socialize. It's more fun than making money should be. Visit *www.sidetick.com*

75. **Make existing software better.** There are many types of software out there that need to be tweaked in order to make it better. You can do just that. If you're good and can make it better, you can make a decent amount of money.

ADVERTISING & AFFILIATE MARKETING

76. **Start up with ClickBank.** If you're looking for a way to get started making money as an affiliate, *www.ClickBank.com* can be one of the most cost effective ways to get started. The affiliate account is free with this site and you'll have literally thousands of products to choose to promote.

77. **Market CPA Offers.** You're not going to have to be an accountant to make this one work, but it is through your online advertising which encourages people to buy a product that you will make money. The downside is that you will have to have a website or blog that you're already working on. This might tie in well with making a website for a special niche.

78. **Work through Google AdSense.** If you have a website for a niche, such as your gardening website, you can use Google AdSense to place topic specific ads on your site. When people click on those ads from your site, you make money. Get a large enough following and you might find that you make a decent amount of money at it. Visit *www.google.com/adsense*

79. **Consider networking or MLM marketing.** This is known as multi level marketing and is also called networking, and you'll be promoting and selling a product through this type money making opportunity. Just make sure that you believe in what you're promoting and be ready to network like crazy. This

means lots of time on your computer. If you're diligent though, you might find that this really pays off for you.

80. **Work with the Amazon Associates program.** This is another type of affiliate marketing that you might want to try. You get to direct customers to your recommended products and make money when they buy them. Visit *affiliate-program.amazon.com*

81. **Become a Domain Registrar Reseller.** This is essentially just a referral service, but it can be relatively simple to do. If you've ever bought a domain name, then you found a domain registrar. Essentially, you're sending customers to a domain registrar and when they buy a domain, you get some of the proceeds.

82. **Post product reviews on your blog.** If you have a blog and you want to make a little extra money, you might want to consider doing this. Keep it ethical and don't claim that you've used a product you haven't. Instead, talk about the product and what you might do with it or how it might work for you. Check out *PayPerPost.com* to get started.

83. **Use your blog to promote companies that you're familiar with.** This often works well if you have companies that are looking to start up a solid online presence. They pay you to promote them, or give you a discount on services. Think HVAC care – you give them free advertising, they give you a discount. Sometimes they will pay you and sometimes you can negotiate discounts, which add up to saving money.

84. **Sell ad space from your website.** If you have a special niche website, you can sell some space of your website and make money. It will help your niche site generate income and is easy to do. Check out *BuySellAds.com* to get started.

85. **Work the stock market.** Okay, so you might kind of be considered to be a day trader, but you don't have to be so high risk about things if you don't want to. You will have to have your own start up funds and have some knowledge, but this is a good way to make a little – or a lot of extra money. One of the best online stock resources is *Etrade.com*.

86. **Answer surveys.** Now some of these might not offer you anything, but most of the time you will find that you can enjoy rewards such as discounts at your favorite store, gift cards, rewards and even cash. Some sites enter you to win and others will pay you when you follow a few simple steps. Just be certain that you don't have to order anything that you don't want and you might find that this is a great way to enjoy some extras. Check out *MyOpinionNow.com* as just one way to get started.

87. **Sign up for a money saving website.** Sites such as *Ebates.com* and MyPoints.com are two places where you'll find you can make some money – on your purchases, that is. My Points lets you earn points every time you purchase through their participating retailers and Ebates offers you cash on your purchases. The great news is that there are lots of retailers that participate on these websites so no matter what you need you can find it through one of the retailers on these sites. Consider doing all of your holiday and birthday shopping on these sites and you'll find you get a nice little bonus for yourself.

88. **Submit your creative fiction for writing contests – and win.** Well, maybe you'll win, but some of these contests can offer a really nice sized bonus for you.

Plus, you'll enjoy recognition that comes with it such as being featured in a publication. You'll find lots of writing contests out there, but some are more elite than others, so dust off your best work, edit it again and see if you can't win.

89. **The same goes with your poetry.** Poetry is subjective. A byline in poetry might not mean much on your resume, but in some contests you can win big, so it's worth it if you've got some good stuff.

90. **Become a FOREX trader.** This isn't something that a newbie would want to invest a lot in, but if you're really into trading, you can really make a lot of money doing this type of trading. Make sure that you educate yourself well before you start out, though. Visit *forex.com*

91. **Enter online sweepstakes / contests.** It's a reach, but not always totally out of the water for many people. About.com (*http://contests.about.com/*) is one of the best known sites for finding current sweepstakes. The prizes can be very large, but remember that your chances for winning are pretty slim. Lots of people are entering online contests and winning all kinds of things. Depending on your luck and what you win, you might be able to turn around and re-sell it.

92. **Play online games.** Whether you find that you're good at online poker or slots, you can win lots of money when you know how to play the right way. Just make sure to set a solid budget, look for the best bonuses and don't go over your personal edge. If you happen to have an additive personality, you might want to stay away from this method and opt for sweepstakes instead. That way, you don't risk losing money (as most sweepstakes are free to enter).

93. **If you're musical, why not make it and sell it?**
Check out sites like CraigsList.org to see how many
musicians are looking for great songs to perform. Are
you an aspiring producer or composer? List your
tunes on *AudioJungle.net* and get paid for the music you
make.

94. **Write grant proposals to pursue what you want to
do.** This is not for the faint of heart, but if you can
identify what you want to do and find sources to help
you out, then you might be onto something. Works
especially well if you need financial assistance for
home repairs, to get an education or want to help
non-profit organizations.

95. **Consider a program such as Project Payday.** This
is a program where you can make a little extra money
if you need to. All you really need to do is sign up for
trials, but you have to make sure that you cancel them
in time or the money you make will go out in the
payments of the things you sign up for. It's said to be
boring, but when you're looking to make some
money, it might be worth it.

96. **Have an online yard sale with CraigsList.** This is a
great way to sell the things you have in your home that
you no longer use. Baby stuff goes great, but you
might find that you can sell nearly everything. Make
sure to get great photos and consider learning a little
bit about SEO to help make your listings go well.

97. **Write greeting cards.** This might or might not make
you some money, depending on what you have in
mind, but there are many greeting card companies that
do accept submissions. You should know that many
times, your verse will have to go through a screening
process, so this isn't quick money, but it's a solid way
to get going in the field.

98. **Cash in on pod casts.** If you have a great speaking voice, you can create pod casts on all kinds of topics and sell them for money through sponsorship opportunities. This is a lot like narrating a story, so you'll have to be expressive, speak clearly and fluidly and not sound as if you're reading from a script.

99. **Sell your art – on the internet.** If you're the artistic type and have lots of artwork lying around, consider marketing it online. In an effort to make home look homier and style life, many people are seeking artwork, but if it's too expensive, they might not buy. Artists just starting out can start up a website and sell their wares to more people than imaginable. Visit *ArtFire.com or redbubble.com*

100. **Create scrapbooking templates.** Now, this might count as a service, but the bottom line is that if you're good, you can make up templates for scrapbooking and sell them for really great money. Turn it into an eBook and make even more.

101. **You can read other people's emails for pay.** Lots of big companies can't do it themselves, so they outsource the work. Pay depends on what you read, but you can make some money on this. Check out a site like *SendEarnings.com* to find out if this suits you.

ABOUT THE AUTHOR

L.L. Maiden is an author and online entrepreneur. She is the owner of www.BlackGuidetoMoney.com, a leading online publication and resource for people of color. Over the past 5 years, she has owned over 20 online companies. Her businesses have been featured in Black Enterprise as well as several other publications. Maiden's businesses expand globally, as she has worked with clients in: Spain, Nigeria, Australia, China, Germany, Kenya, Malaysia, Finland, Puerto Rico, France, Sweden, Canada, Denmark, India, and the United Kingdom. Maiden holds a Bachelor of Arts from Spelman College. She currently resides in Atlanta, GA.

For more resources, check out www.BlackGuidetoMoney.com

BLACK GUIDE to *Money*